Jennifr

Emily Carr

CANADIAN
STARTERS

GLC 115 Nugget Avenue, Agincourt, Ontario M1S 3B1 (416) 291-2926

About Starters

Starters books are written and designed with young readers in mind. They are vocabulary controlled and the contents have been carefully checked by a critic reader and teacher panel.

Each book contains questions for teacher-directed learning, bright and simple illustrations, interesting and informative text, picture glossary and a table of facts.

ISBN 0-88874-331-9

Edited by: GLC Editorial Department
Illustrations: Carlos Freire, Grafika Art Studios
Critic Reader: Mrs. Margaret Knechtel, Reading Consultant,
Etobicoke Board of Education
Teacher Panel: Miss Grace Davis, Grade 2 Teacher,
John D. Parker Junior Public School,
Etobicoke Board of Education
Miss Maribel Hanson, Grade 2 Teacher,
Buttonwood Hill Junior Public School,
Etobicoke Board of Education

Printed by: Ashton-Potter Limited
Film preparation: Graphic Litho-plate Inc.
Bound by: The Hunter Rose Company Ltd.

Printed and Bound in Canada

Uniquely Canadian Materials from GLC Publishers Limited
115 Nugget Avenue
Agincourt, Ontario

...ese people are looking at
...famous Canadian painting.
...was painted by Emily Carr.
...mily lived in the province of British Columbia.

Emily was born in the city of Victoria.
She was nicknamed "Small" by her older sisters.
Her mother and father died while she was still
a young girl.

2

Emily always loved to draw.
She made herself an easel.
She liked to be alone.

3

Emily wanted to go to art school.
So she was sent to San Francisco.
Emily could learn about art in San Francisco.

4

mily learned to paint many things.
ie studied for five years.

Emily returned to Victoria.
She set up her own studio.
She taught children how to paint.

6

One summer Emily lived in an Indian village.
She admired the Indian way of life.
They loved nature.

7

Emily wanted to learn more about art.
She decided to go to England.

8

mily did not like England,
ut she enjoyed her art classes.
he worked so hard that she became ill.

9

She was so ill that she could not draw.
When she felt better, she returned to Canada.

here were many Indians in British Columbia.
ey lived in small villages.
ch village had totem poles.

Emily visited the villages every summer.
She wanted to draw the totem poles.

he Indians no longer carved them.

he knew that soon there would be no more

tem poles.

There was a new way of painting in France.
Emily wanted to go there to learn about it.

14

mily and her sister went to France.

France she painted many pictures.

me were put on display.

There was nothing more left to learn.
The two sisters set out for home.
Emily was anxious to paint
Indian villages again.

er paintings filled her studio.

o one liked them.

o one wanted her to teach art.

She built a house and rented out part of it.

She was a good landlady.

She learned to take care of the house herself.

mily no longer painted.

he had to find a way to make money.

he made pottery, raised sheepdogs,

id learned to weave.

The National Gallery learned about
Emily's paintings.
Her paintings went on exhibit in Toronto.
Emily travelled to Toronto to see the exhibit.

20

he met many artists and saw many paintings.

he met the Canadian artists known as

e Group of Seven.

mily wanted to start painting again.

Emily loved the west coast forest of Canada.
She moved so she could be near it.
She painted many pictures of the forest.

22

ther artists came to see Emily.

er paintings became known

round the world.

any of her paintings were sold.

Emily became ill.

She could not paint so she began to write.

She wrote about her life.

One of her books won an award.

he continued to write and to paint

ntil her death.

oday her paintings are very valuable.

Picture Glossary

easel
(page 3)

National Gallery
(page 20)

studio
(page 6)

exhibit
(page 20)

village
(page 11)

Group of Seven
(page 21)

totem pole
(page 11)

west coast forest
(page 22)

RIVERDALE SCHOOL